Growing Up:
Our Childhood Survival Guide

James Selvy

Wolfpac Books

Published by Wolfpac Books LLC

Copyright © 2025 by Wolfpac Books LLC

All rights reserved.

Copyright registration pending with the U.S. Copyright Office.

Growing Up: Our Childhood Survival Guide

by James Selvy

1st Edition | Arizona: Wolfpac Books, 2025

ISBN 978-1-968443-04-7 (eBook)

ISBN 978-1-968443-05-4 (Paperback)

ISBN 978-1-968443-06-1 (Hardback)

DEDICATION

To Mom and Dad,

Thanks for letting us stumble, fumble, and occasionally face-plant through childhood. Your trust in our ability to learn from our messes shaped this book—and us. With love and laughter.

PREFACE

My name is Jim, and the oldest of three boys. My brothers, Don and Ron, were twins born just shy of thirteen months after me. Some people even thought we were triplets.

We had lots of adventures growing up. It was a different time back then. We'd race our motorcycles through dusty trails, hunt and catch lizards, only dashing home for a quick sandwich before tearing back out until the street lights turned on. There were no cell phones. Our parents gave us guidelines on where we could and couldn't go. We were instructed to stay together. Most days, they had no clue if we were chasing lizards in the field or racing bikes down dusty trails. But they trusted us, and we knew one wrong move could trap us indoors, doing chores instead of having fun.

My Dad was a character. His gravelly voice roared orders like a grizzly, but his teddy-bear heart shone when he quietly fixed our neighbor Olive's roof. After a shady contractor scammed the widow next door, Dad came home every night for a week, hammering and sealing until sunset, never telling a soul outside the family. He always said 'good works' don't need a spotlight.

In 2015, just before Thanksgiving, Dad passed away at the age of 81. He made the staff and us laugh as they rolled him into surgery. He had been sick for a while, but we hoped that the surgery would get him back to health. He never woke up from surgery. At the funeral, once all of the scheduled activities were completed, we asked our friends and family to tell stories about Dad.

Most of the stories revolved around our family and our adventures. The church echoed with laughter as family, friends, and neighbors swapped tales of our scrapes, their voices glowing with nostalgia. A surprising number revolved around life-and-death situations. Looking back, it is those stories that prompted the creation of this collection. Don't worry, not all are life-and-death, but there are more than you might think. Most are humorous when viewed in retrospect. Some of our antics were risky—don't try them at home! Instead, we hope you laugh and learn from our mistakes. These mistakes made us into the men we are today.

These stories, told by Jim, Don, and Ron, are based on our childhood. We even have a few from Mom. We reminisced and picked a few of our favorites. They are in no particular order, each from our own perspective. We hope they make you smile as they do us.

Acknowledgements

My deepest gratitude goes to my Mom, Sharon to the rest of the world, whose vivid memories and heartfelt stories breathed life into this memoir. Her uncanny ability to recall the wild, joyful chaos of our childhood adventures, with every detail as fresh as yesterday, shaped these stories into something truly special.

I'm equally thankful for my brothers Don and Ron, whose hilarious and heartfelt contributions added layers of laughter and warmth to these pages. Their knack for unearthing those long-buried escapades—especially the mischievous ones we kept from Mom for decades—brought back floods of memories and endless chuckles.

This journey is a truly a family affair, turning our individual recollections into a shared tapestry of love, laughter, and lessons. This book wouldn't be what it is without your voices woven into every story.

CONTENTS

Epigraph

Surviving chaos with kin, we grew fearless,
ready for life's next leap.

BOAT SUNK - JIM

This is one of my favorite stories. I was a kid in elementary school. We often went to Okemah Lake[1] to fish, water ski, and swim. The old part, quiet with anglers casting line, was for fishing only, while the new part roared with fast boats and laughter. A spillway separated them. We lived for those summers, catching fish and skiing every weekend, and this Saturday was no different.

The boat ramp was at the beginning of the spillway on the old lake. The spillway, a brick wall barrier, divided the old lake from the new one. The brick wall was knocked down between the two lakes to allow boat traffic between the lates. Dark water churned below, dropping off sharply. Arriving just before lunch, we shoved the boat into the water, its hull scraping the rocky floor, tugged it along the ramp, then tied it up to a tree before eating.

Mom's rule felt like gospel: no swimming for 30 minutes after eating to prevent cramps. She'd wag her finger, her voice firm, while we fidgeted, eyeing the lake. No internet back then, so we couldn't check her claim.

After the restriction lifted, we donned swimsuits, grabbed towels, and returned to ski. The boat sagged low, water sloshing in its stern, while the bow rested high on the shore. Dad checked the boat's switch and saw the plug hanging on it. "Damn it, we forgot to put the plug in. What do we do now? We can't pull it up on shore enough to drain it." He rubbed his forehead, pacing, as I watched the lake lap at the hull. This boat had two plugs: one inside to drain splash water, and another screw-in below the waterline. We forgot about the screw-in.

As was often the case, Grandpa and Dad debated what to do. The boat, too heavy with water, couldn't be trailered but being beached, it wouldn't sink.

Grandpa suggested, "Put the plug in, back out, get it up on plane, then have Jim pull it. Water'll flow out. Replug it, then trailer to drain the rest." Dad nodded. They had a plan. Mom's lips tightened, her eyes darting to the water, but she said nothing, deferring to her dad.

I put on a life jacket, inserted the inside plug, and pushed off. Dad started the motor and reversed. About twenty feet out, the boat began to roll. It was going to flip, and we couldn't stop it.

"Jim, jump!" Dad shouted. I climbed and perched on the edge. I hesitated, my heart pounding, eyes locked on his tense grip on the wheel. When the boat was on its side, he yelled again, "Jump!". I jumped, plunging underwater and then quickly back to the surface. The boat soon flipped upside down.

Floating in the water, I searched for Dad. The lake's surface stayed unbroken where he should've been. He wasn't a strong swimmer. I saw Mom pacing the shoreline, her eyes searching the water. She shouted, "Where is he? Is he trapped?" Thirty seconds felt eternal.

The boat, fully inverted, stayed afloat. Dad finally surfaced, and I let out a relieved breath. I heard Mom shout from shore, "What were you doing? We thought you were trapped!"

"I waited for the boat to stabilize. Swam out between the canopy arms."

I don't recall how we righted or trailered the boat. But once on the trailer, we saw water flowing from the bilge out of the screw-in plug. Water had rushed through the forgotten screw-in plug into the bilge, shifting the boat's balance and causing it to capsize.

Some items had floated to the surface, while others were lost to the depths of the lake. But Dad and I were safe, and the boat was recovered. Exhausted, we slumped on the shore, Mom hugging us tightly. Months passed, but the lake had one last surprise.

The following spring, Mom's sister-in-law called Dad. "Did you lose a green military jacket?"

"Maybe. Why?"

"On Easter, I was fishing on the spillway. Snagged something heavy—a green military jacket. 'Selvy' was inked on the neck. Figured it's yours. I was fishing right where your boat sank."

"Right! It was in the front storage of the boat. Must've floated out when it flipped and stayed on the bottom of the lake."

Years later, I checked out Mom's no-swimming-after-eating rule. We followed it without question, but it's a myth.[2] Swimming after eating does not increase drowning risk. Sorry Mom.

No Brakes - Jim

It is hot in Arizona. My family and I tried to find places close to home to escape the heat. We discovered a small lake, measuring 11 acres, which I considered a pond, located at the top of Mount Graham within the Coronado National Forest. It was stocked with brown and brook trout. The real draw was that while the elevation at the base was 3000 feet, Riggs Lake was at 8600. Much cooler than the Sonoran Desert we lived in. There are only 31 campsites, so it does not get too many campers.

We went here often with some family friends. The next chapter is another story narrated by Ron and set at the Lake, but this one is my story about about our RV.

At this time, we had an old RV, similar to a Winnebago. It was ancient, bought from the estate of a man who drowned in Roosevelt Lake. The RV was filthy and poorly maintained. It took us months to get it livable and drivable.

Our climb up the mountain started smoothly. The road wound up the mountain, slowing to 25 mph at sharp turns, with no guardrail for most of the way and only a few pullouts to stop. If you left the road, it was a long, sharp drop to the desert floor.

As we approached the lake, the brake light came on. I watched Dad check the parking brake; no issue there. The RV responded, slowing under Dad's steady pressure on the brake pedal. I hoped the brake issue needed only some fluid. Since Dad couldn't fix the brakes then, and we were nearly there, we continued on to the campsite for him to check later.

Dad always had his toolbox and assorted fluids in all of his vehicles, and the RV was no exception. Once camp was set, I helped him pull out his tools. I saw him open the hood. He spent hours testing the RV's electrical systems and checking the fluids and brakes.

He closed the hood, packed his tools, and we headed out to fish. That trip stayed with me, the taste of fresh fish for dinner and gooey s'mores by our campfire lingering in my mind. When the weekend ended, we packed up and started down the mountain.

As we wound down the mountain, I overheard Mom ask Dad, "So did you fix it?" Why's she asking now, when we're already descending? I wondered.

Dad replied with a simple, "Yup."

When Mom pressed further, "So what was it?"

He shrugged, "Don't know."

Looking at Mom's face, I saw the color drain from her face. "What do you mean you don't know?"

"I couldn't find anything wrong, so I cut the wire to the warning lamp."

Mom froze, her voice trembling as she stammered, "So what happens if the brakes fail? We won't be able to stop." We're gonna launch off this mountain like RV version of Dukes of Hazzard, I thought, heart pounding.

"Already talked with Lou. He is driving in front of us. If there is a problem, I will push the side of the RV into the side of the mountain to slow us down. Lou will slow his rig down in front of us and use his brakes to stop us. It'll be ok. Let me focus on the road." Mom's hands gripped the seat, her face pale and unconvinced.

My pulse raced, envisioning us as a headline on the nightly news, yet we made it down safely, no issues.

Once home, I saw Dad tinkering with the RV's engine again. I'm unsure if Dad fixed a brake issue or left the warning lamp wire cut.

STRANGER'S RV - RON

On our late summer RV camping trip, we joined family friends at Riggs Lake, a small mountain lake too tiny for boats, where we kept busy with fishing, hiking, and evening campfires with nearby campers. So, I figured there were probably people around that I didn't know, but who were still somehow attached to our group. On the night in question, the area was busy because it was a long weekend. We had met some of our family friends and, as I recall, some friends of friends at a site with concrete tables and fire pits, where everyone set up dinner and shared food. There were plenty of other groups doing the same, and vehicles were lined up along the site.

Things were going well, and it was just about time to eat when a light sprinkle kissed my face, others glancing warily skyward, sensing a storm. The rain intensified, and people began edging toward sheltered areas by vehicle or even just under substantial trees, but there was still hope that it was a passing shower. A brilliant flash seared the sky, thunder crashing instantly, rain unleashing a torrent, sending everyone scrambling for shelter. I froze for a second, then, after the momentary flash blindness had subsided, all I saw in the rainy darkness was people running everywhere. Two strangers dashed past, diving into a warmly lit camper. Assuming they were with our group, I slipped in behind. I closed the door behind me and looked at a young couple who turned around after just running in and were surprised to see me.

The woman said, "Hello. Do we know you?"

I said, "I don't think so. Are you with the (one of the families we were with)?" The rain was pouring down outside.

"No," she said, paused, and said, "Well, do you want some steak?" I noticed they had some steaks on a plate that they had carried in with them. When I agreed, she fixed me a plate and said, "As soon as this rain lets up a little, we should find your parents."

We sat down, and I heard a knock on the door. The guy in the camper opened it and said, "Are you looking for a boy?" I listened to a voice agree, and they said, "Well, we're feeding him! Come on in!"

I forgot whether it was my mother or father, but the caller arrived, and everyone met each other. We made another camping buddy! The steak was also quite good.

LOST IN WOODS - JIM

I remember when our neighbor Andy, about our age, got a mini-bike. The mini-bike's engine roared, its sleek frame gleaming under the sun, and my brothers and I couldn't stop staring. Andy was in a wheelchair. Andy ended up in a wheelchair because of a drunk driver. The crash stole his parents and left him unable to walk from the waist down. Of course, the drunk driver suffered no permanent injuries. That tragedy etched itself into my heart, strengthening my vow never to drive intoxicated.

They took the mini-bike down to the woods after dinner. It was still light, but shadows lengthened across the trail. His grandparents, who had taken responsibility for Andy, asked if we wanted to go along. YES.

My brothers and I pedaled our bikes to the woods, grins wide, hearts racing with anticipation. Andy's sister had the engine running, waiting for Andy. The mini-bike's headlight cast a glowing path across the bridge from the parking lot into the woods.

Andy was lifted onto the back and gripped his sister tightly. She took off across the bridge. The bike's rumble echoed through the trees, pulling me in. That looks fun. I'm going too.

I shot a glance at my brothers, "You guys stay here." Stupid idea looking back. She didn't know I was following, and her speed left my pedaling in the dust.

No surprise what came next. Just read the chapter title, I got lost.

As the sun set, the woods swallowed all light, trees blocking any hint of moon or stars. My teeth chattered in the biting cold. My heart pounded, fear clawing at my chest. And it was getting darker. No one knew where I was, I had no flashlight, and cell phones hadn't been invented yet.

I could've slumped to the ground, tears flowing from my eyes to the dusty ground. I certainly thought about it, but that wasn't productive. The trail I'd followed had twisted into a maze. Even in grade school, I knew I had to act. Clenching my fists, I resolved to push on. My goal was to get out of the woods.

I inched forward, hands outstretched, trying to stay on a straight path. It was agonizingly slow because darkness hid every step. Eventually, I stumbled out into a vast, unfamiliar field.

Far to the left, I pictured the park near the library, but it was too distant. I'd never make it. Besides, no lights beckoned. The moon was bright, not quite full, but its glow revealed patches of grass and jutting rocks.

To the right, a faint light flickered. I couldn't read it, but I recognized the shape and colors—a Sinclair gas station sign, maybe a mile off. It was my North Star, the moon lighting my way.

I don't remember the journey across that field. All I remember is locking my gaze on that gas sign, each step driven by the promise of a phone.

I'm writing this, so clearly I didn't die in the woods or field. I rolled into the gas station, legs trembling, and found the attendant. He called my parents, his calm voice assuring them I was safe. He must've shared the address, because they came and got me and my bike.

From what Don and Ron later shared, Andy's family didn't know what to do, so they just returned home, bringing my brothers with them. I can't believe it. They had a mini-bike with a headlight. They could've searched, and maybe they did.

But I was still a small boy, alone in the dark woods. It taught me to not panic and look for solutions.

MOTORCYCLES - JIM

When we lived in Oklahoma in grade school, my Dad had a Yamaha 350 street motorcycle that he used to commute to work. Not sure how they came up with the idea or why, but my parents got us a used motorcycle for Christmas. It was a yellow Yamaha 60cc mini enduro. Lots of people think of mini-bikes. This was an actual dirt bike, albeit smaller in size than what you might picture. As a young boy, I was in heaven.

They would take us down to the parking lot of the high school down the street to practice stop-and-go, only in first gear. Eventually, we graduated to riding with Dad in the woods next to the high school.

Having only one motorcycle was frustrating, but at least we had one. A few months later, they purchased another one, the same model and color. Again, later on, we got a third one, the same model, same color. So we all had one now. We each picked one to be our own personal motorcycle.

Dad rode with us. I know it was hard on his street bike in the dirt, but at least we're doing something together. He was able to keep an eye on us and ensure we were being safe. Mom didn't want to be left out when Dad and the boys went for a ride. They ended up getting her a Yamaha Enduro 125cc. She strapped a plastic milk crate to the back and put her miniature dachshund, Tina, in it. It still amazes me to this day that Tina stayed in the basket. The only time I saw Tina jump out was when Mom fell over one time. Tina waited until the bike was almost on th ground, and then she just hopped out, as if she knew what she was doing. Mom was not as adventurous as her boys, but she was with us. How many moms do you know who would go out in the dirt and ride motorcycles with her boys? I have never met one.

One of the unexpected benefits we didn't consider at the time was learning about engines. All mechanical devices require regular maintenance. We learned how to fill it with gas, change the oil, and replace the gas filter. Sometimes, more complex work was needed. Dad would tear into it, and we would help him. Mostly, we just handed him tools and such, but it was a bonding and learning experience.

The training did not end when we got to the dirt. Once in the dirt, he taught us how to shift to higher gears and downshift. We didn't know it at the time, but this would make it easier when we learned to drive a car for the first time. Dad was determined to have us learn on a car with a stick shift before we graduated to an automatic. The motorcycle and the car had different ways to shift, but the experience of when to shift up and down gears and using a clutch was familiar.

Of course, being young and fearless, we were more adventurous than our parents. We became more confident and capable riders. They allowed us to explore the capabilities of our motorcycle and to always think about safety. To be honest, the safety was not as important as pushing the envelope and having fun. I was a bit of a thrill seeker.

Before we had achieved confidence in our skills, we would ride over this little bump in the field. We were cautioned not to go too fast, so we would stay on the ground, or at least that was the intention. I don't know exactly what happened, except that Ron went too fast and got airborne. He claimed it was not intentional, and I believe him. Because when in mid-air, he hit the kill switch. This switch shuts off electricity to the engine, effectively turning off the motorcycle. It was to be used when getting off the bike, think turning off the switch on a car. Using the switch mid-air was not the best plan. He landed, crashed, and, believe it or not, got only a few scrapes.

Don and I thought it was cool. It was not too long before all three of us were using the hill to jump in the air on purpose. We learned to ensure that the front tire stayed a bit higher than the rear, and the engine remained on just like the professionals on TV. Good Times.

By the time we moved to Arizona, I was starting Junior High. We had been riding our motorcycles for a while by then. Mom and Dad bought a house with a wash behind it. The wash was connected with several big fields. The wash allowed us to access the fields without having to go on the streets. However, to reach the fields, we had to cross the street. The street had a bridge with a culvert for water from the wash. This culvert had two sides. We always used the one on the south side. It was taller. On our small motorcycles and as kids, it allowed us to ride our motorcycles in the upright position without having to duck.

My brothers and I always went to the field together. By this time, our parents let us go by ourselves. They knew our abilities, we were together in case there was an issue (remember no cell phones), and we didn't have to get on any streets. I don't recall how it happened, but on this day, I was alone. I suspect my brothers had already gone home, and I came home late for some reason.

I was stupid. I thought, I am going to take the other culvert. I am sure I can do it. What is the worst that can happen? Just some advice, if you have to talk yourself into something using this logic, you're asking for trouble. I soon learned.

Everything was going well. I leaned forward as I made my way down the culvert. But it was getting shorter and shorter. My head hit the cement on the top of the culvert. I tried to lower my head, but I had no luck. I was thinking so much about the helmet, I forgot about the throttle. As I continued forward, my head rolled back. As my head rolled back, my hand on the throttle also rolled back, increasing the speed. The motorcycle shot forward out of the culvert. I fell on my back. My helmet hit the ground.

As I lay there taking an assessment, my back hurt. I later found out it was all scraped up. When I tried to get up, I couldn't. My body would not respond. I have broken my neck. I am paralyzed. No one knows I am here. I wonder how long before someone finds me. Mom and Dad are going to kill me because I did something so stupid.

I lay there for about five minutes. My motorcycle was on its side, idling in the wash. I was able to finally crawl out of the culvert and pull my bike upright. My neck was killing me, but at least I was moving. I got the bike on the alleyway running behind the houses by the wash and walked my motorcycle home.

My shirt was torn, my back bloody, my helmet all scratched, but I was alive and moving. I never took that culvert again.

FENCE ZAP - MOM

I'm the non-helicopter mom of three boys. I learned from the best, as my mom and dad were non-helicopter parents. I grew up drinking from the hose, playing outside with friends until dark, climbing trees, and playing in the mud. Mom and Dad loved me. They cheered my scraped knees from tree-climbing, tossing me a bandage with a grin, trusting I'd figure it out. The following story shows that my dad continued his parenting philosophy into my adulthood.

Mom and Dad had a home in the country outside of Oklahoma City. They had a few acres to develop, and they even had space for a couple of horses. They lived just a few miles from us. Our family, my Mom and

Dad, and my brother's clan each staked our garden plots, crowing over whose tomatoes grew juiciest or whose okra stood tallest.

After wrangling my elementary students all day, I'd wander the property, the scent of fresh earth and distant horse manure easing my mind under the Oklahoma sunset.

Mom and Dad loved for the families to come over and tend their gardens, visit, and ride the horses. The boys and their cousins ran wild, climbed trees, and claimed their own spot called Pleasant Gardens.

One evening, as I strolled, I found my husband, Don, and Dad working on a fence. Dad and Don rarely worked together because their stubborn streaks clashed. They were bending over discussing what they were doing. I grinned, watching them swap ideas over the fence without their usual bickering.

While I was visiting with them, I bent down, checked out the project, and reached for the repair on the fence. Don opened his mouth to warn me, but Dad shot him a sly glance, shaking his head with a smirk.

I touched the fence and got a shock right down to my toes! It was an electric fence! Dad used me to test if it was working!! I yelped, stumbling back as the jolt zapped through me! My husband and father watched me get shocked!!

I couldn't believe they conspired to shock me! How could they do that to me?! I was their wife and daughter! I thought they loved me! They doubled over, cackling, slapping each other's backs like they'd won a prank championship! They were thrilled their repair worked! Did they think that I would laugh and walk away?

Oh yes, they both paid for that stunt! Did they care? Nope!! Don was happy that he and my dad actually worked together, shared a secret, and a good laugh. Dad was a non-helicopter parent who let his daughter learn from experience.

Suckers - Jim

Grandpa was great. He took us fishing and pulled us with his boat to water ski. But his eyes twinkled with mischief when he teased us, especially during our battles with Oklahoma's bloodsucking creatures.

We spent a great deal of time at the lake and playing in the grass. Oklahoma bugs and mosquitoes were nasty, but more problematic were the numerous ticks and chiggers. You've probably heard of the blood sucking ticks, but chiggers are a species of mite you may not know—a close relative to spiders and ticks.

I'll cover chiggers later, but first let's talk about ticks. Brushing through tall grass, we'd find these ninja spiders climbing up our jeans, to bury their tiny heads into our skin, bloating like little vampires. There was no pain, so unless I happened to see them or feel a strange lump under my shirt, itching faintly, they'd suck me dry. I have seen them swell up to the size of a small marble, YUCK.

Once found, it was a challenge to get them off. The first instinct was to grab their body and pull. But yanking an engorged tick often leaves its head behind, a recipe for infection. Therefore, the best scenario is to encourage the parasite to do so of its own accord. Of course, it's feasting happily, so asking nicely is rarely effective.

Grandpa had an answer for everything. He smoked a pipe at the time, so he had a plethora of matches. He'd strike one, let it flare, then blow it out, pressing the hot match head to the tick's body with a steady hand, grinning as I squirmed. My heart raced, fearing he'd slip and burn my skin. More often than not, this worked. This was an uncomfortable procedure, but nothing compared to the chiggers.

You might not know, but like ticks, chiggers like to live in the tall grass. But unlike ticks, they are VERY SMALL, microscopic, and almost invisible to the naked eye. The freeloaders hitch a ride on socks or waistbands, targeting tight spots like a covert invasion. They swarm warm, tight places, leaving trails of fiery welts. The tiny torture villains attach to clothing and move to feed on skin, often in areas where clothing is the tightest, such as socks and underwear. The itch is relentless, a burning prickle, like tiny fires under the skin.

I slathered Calamine lotion on my legs and stomach, turning pink as bubblegum, but the relief was fleeting. But Grandpa had a different idea.

He'd grab Grandma's hairspray can, muttering, "Gotta force those buggers out," and douse my red, itchy welts. The stuff that made hair stick together would seal off their air, he'd claim with a smirk.

The problem was that hairspray contained alcohol. The spray hit like a swarm of bees, stinging my young, tender skin, sending me hopping and yelping across the yard. He would laugh as I danced in agony, his pipe puffing smoke while he clapped, but his grin showed he cared. I guess the alcohol did help to prevent infection, but chiggers loved underwear, the worst spot for a boy to feel that fiery sting.

Years later, I looked up chiggers. Reading and scratching a long-gone itch, I learned that they do not burrow; instead, they pierce the skin and inject saliva that liquefies cells into a mushy food source. Those now-liquid cells are sucked up as food.[1]

It is even worse than burrowing into the skin. Chiggers are one reason I now live in Arizona. No chiggers here.

FRIDGE DUMP - JIM

Easter sun beat down as we camped at
Apache Lake, 65 miles northeast of Phoenix,
near Roosevelt's shimmering waters. Our
pickup camper's tight quarters squeezed
us in. Mom and Dad sprawled across the
overhead bed, while my brothers and I
wrestled for space on a table-turned-bed
and a narrow fold-down bunk. When
Mom's cooking filled the air with sizzling
bacon, we'd stumble out, elbows bumping,
to sprawl on lawn chairs or splash in the
lake until dinner called.

That Easter, the sun scorched Apache
Lake, my skin prickling red under its
glare. Ignorant of sunblock's future shield, I
winced as my shoulders burned. To escape

the heat, we dashed into the lake, splashing wildly, only to shiver in water so cold it stole my breath, likely from Roosevelt Dam's icy spill.

Easter morning, Mom and Dad scattered eggs across the sandy shore. Being in Junior High, my brothers and I rolled our eyes, too old for such games, but we still raced across the dunes, kicking up sand, laughing as we unearthed each colored prize.

We packed up, cramming gear into the camper's tight corners, each item wedged into its spot to avoid chaos. I glanced at the refrigerator, its door shut but latch loose, a mistake I'd only realize in a few short moments.

The narrow two-lane road twisted through the canyon's steep walls. My brothers and I sprawled on the overhead bed, eyes tracing the rugged cliffs outside. Suddenly, the refrigerator door swung open, ketchup bottles and water jugs clattering to the floor. The worst was the creamed corn, its slimy globs mingling with orange juice, flowing like a sickly yellow chemical spill. My stomach churned at the sight, like the aftermath of a bad flu, almost causing me to vomit and add to the disaster. The mess was spreading with each turn of the road.

I crawled down, knees bumping the narrow walls, and yanked open the small window to the truck. "Mom, the refrigerator opened—orange juice and corn are everywhere. We need to stop!"

Mom peeked through, eyes wide, and spun to Dad. "We need to stop!" Her words sliced through the camper's hum as she glared at me. "Jim, close the refrigerator so nothing else spills."

I clambered across the cabinets avoiding the floor, slammed the door shut, and clicked the lock, my nose wrinkling at the sticky mess still pooling below.

Dad's knuckles whitened on the steering wheel, his eyes locked on the twisting road. "No place to pull over. It'll have to wait," he snapped, the truck rumbling on. My gut tightened, the mess flowing in waves.

For at least 15 minutes, the camper lurched along, no shoulder wide enough to stop. My brothers and I huddled on the overhead bed, legs dangling, hemmed in by the stench below. Once stopped, Mom cracked the door, revealing a floor coated in slimy corn and juice, smeared evenly by the road's relentless curves.

Dad found a shoulder to pull off on. Dad's voice boomed through the open window, sharp against the canyon's echo. "We can't stay here. We have to get moving!"

Mom snatched up sealed ketchup bottles and water jugs, shoving them back into the fridge. Empty containers clattered into the sink. She yanked the broom from the closet, sweeping the sour, orange-tinged sludge out the door, its stench stinging my nose. With a quick glance at the mess, she darted back to the truck's front seat.

Back home, the camper's floor clung to our shoes with a tacky grip, leaving a sour reek of orange juice and corn. I scrubbed with a mop, water sloshing, until the stickiness faded. We propped open the windows to air out the stubborn citrus scent for hours. My fingers lingered on the refrigerator latch, checking it twice with a grimace.

BACKYARD GOLF - DON

Growing up, Ron and I fancied ourselves quite the athletes, even if our sports were more... creative than conventional. Our backyard was a stadium, a battlefield, and on this particular summer afternoon, a golf course. The rules were loose, the stakes were bragging rights, and the equipment was, well, improvised. Our "golf ball" was a beat-up softball, and "club" a Louisville Slugger that had seen better days. We'd been at it for hours, hacking away at the poor softball across the patchy grass, dodging flowerbeds, fruit trees, and dogs. By the time we reached the final "hole" (a divot in the dirt), Ron was clearly ahead. I'd lost, and I knew it. But I had one last swing, one final chance to make a statement.

"Well, I can't win," I declared, gripping the bat like I was stepping up to the tee in the PGA Championship, "but I can at least knock it silly."

Ron, ever the competitive show-off, eased up next to me to gloat over his imminent victory. He stood close, too close, as it turned out, grinning as I lined up my shot. I could feel the weight of the moment, the chance to send that softball into orbit, or at least over the neighbor's fence. I drew back, channeling every golf hero I'd ever seen on TV. The swing was perfect: a smooth arc, the bat connecting with a satisfying crack that sent the ball soaring. I followed through with a flourish, marveling at the beauty of the hit, the kind of swing that would've made Babe Ruth nod in approval.

Then, mid-revelry, my swing stopped short. Not because of any fence or tree, but because the bat had found an unexpected target: Ron's forehead. A sickening thwack echoed, followed by a howl that could've woken the dead. "Ow!!!!" Ron yelped, staggering back, his hands clutching his forehead.

I spun around, still clutching the bat, my brain catching up to the disaster. There, on Ron's forehead, was a puffy, red circle, swelling up like a cartoon bump. It was the kind of mark that screamed "emergency room," but we were kids, and our code was clear: tell no one. Snitching meant trouble, and trouble meant no more backyard golf. I stood there, torn between guilt and the urge to laugh at the sheer absurdity of it. Ron, for his part, was glaring at me through watering eyes, muttering something about my aim being worse than my score.

"Sorry, man," I said, trying to sound sincere while biting back a grin. "You weren't supposed to be that close."

He didn't find it funny. Not then, anyway. But the softball was long gone, probably in Mrs. Olive's yard, and Ron's forehead looked like it belonged in a Looney Tunes episode. We swore a pact of silence, sealed with the kind of loyalty only kids understand. No parents, no teachers, no tattling. Just two boys, a bat, and a secret we'd laugh about years later—once the bruise faded, of course. Sorry Mom, this is one of those secrets you only find out when we are all "grown-up".

Spillway Fishing - Jim

I remember one day my brothers and I were standing on the spillway between the old and new parts of Okemah Lake, fishing. I balanced on the crumbling brick spillway, its jagged edge linking muddy shore to man-made peninsula, water roaring through its broken heart, swirling with white foam under a blazing sun, the air thick with the scent of wet moss. I flicked my rod, the line dancing in the breeze, while my brothers cast with steady focus, their gazes fixed on the lake's shimmering green ripples, their soft chuckles mocking my playful antics.

My fingers fumbled, threading five jigs, plastic strips gleaming like bugs, as I ditched the traditional hook. I pressed the button on the reel, and the line sank quickly to the lake bottom, churning up murky silt clouds, veiling the depths.

I reeled slowly, pole arcing downward, battling a lively tug, not a tree branch, but something massive, line whining softly. As the jigs reached the surface, five perch dangled, one on each jig, scales glinting like coins. I nearly toppled off the wall, heart pounding, as I hauled in my prize. I unhooked each perch, its slimy scales slipping in my grip, and dropped them into the rusted metal basket. Each fish had decided to bite my jigs as a last meal. I must have been reeling pretty quickly, though, since one of the fish was not hooked in the mouth, but in its back. Its silvery side flashed, taunting mouth-caught friends, as dragonflies buzzed in the humid air, earning me the title 'Jig Master'.

One day, while fishing on the spillway with Mom and my brothers, I watched Grandpa pull up in his boat. The lake's murky ripples lapped against the shore, the air heavy with the smell of fish and damp earth. He eased in slowly, picked a spot, and headed to the front to drop anchor. Suddenly, he slipped and fell into the water. My grip tightened on the fishing pole, breath catching in my throat. Grandpa wasn't a strong swimmer. I'd never seen him in water over his head, and, of course, he never wore a life jacket.

We were all good swimmers, but when Grandpa sank fast into the deep, murky ripples that swallowed his shadow, I froze. He disappeared completely. Moments later, his head popped up, mouth gaping, eyes darting wildly as he clawed at the water, then sank again.

Mom's voice shook. "What's going on? Where is he?"

Soon, Grandpa surfaced again, eyes bulging as he thrashed for air, only to sink once more. My chest tightened, heart pounding like a drum.

Mom's pole clattered to the ground, her hands fumbling as she leaned toward the water. "Why does he keep going under? What should we do?" She stood, ready to jump in next time.

When Grandpa popped up again, his shoulders relaxed, breath steadying as he clung to the boat's edge. He stayed afloat. We scrambled to help him back onto his boat.

Mom asked, "So, what happened?"

Grandpa, catching his breath, said, "I slipped while holding the anchor. Kept sinking 'cause I was still holding the anchor rope. Let it go the third time, and up I came."

LAKE POWELL – JIM

We headed to Lake Powell in the camper, pulling our motorboat. Lake Powell is huge, with a shoreline of nearly 2,000 miles created by the construction of the Hoover Dam. It stretches from Northern Arizona to southern Utah. It was created by damming up the Colorado River before the Grand Canyon. This lake is so large that it offers houseboat rentals.

We arrived at the lake in the evening, so we set up camp and planned our adventure for the next day. We ate breakfast, loaded the boat with water skis, and packed a picnic lunch. Sweat dripped down my forehead as the lake's shimmering heat baked my skin. We fidgeted, stripping off our shirts, eyes locked on the cool, inviting water. This was the largest body of water we had ever taken the boat on. I don't remember how far we went, but it was far enough that we couldn't see the boat launch anymore. We found a secluded beach, spread out the blanket, pulled out lunch, and bolted for the water.

Once we cooled off enough, we ate our fill at lunch. It was a great morning. Dad and Mom were looking at the clouds, though. Dark clouds swelled ominously. The clouds churned, black as coal, spitting the first heavy drops. It was going to rain. My brothers and I were not too worried. We were in our swimsuits, and a little rain wouldn't hurt.

The wind picked up. You could hear the wind whistling through the canyon. We were protected from most of the wind. Dad said, "I think we need to head back. It's impossible to tell how the wind will affect the wide-open lake. Boys, load up the boat."

We all scrambled to get packed up. We headed back to the boat launch. When we got to the open lake, it was more like an ocean than a lake. The waves were huge. Every summer, we'd hear about boats sinking on Lake Powell. It is a distinctly different experience from what most freshwater boaters are accustomed.

Luckily, the nose of the boat was headed into the waves instead of cross-wise with them. Luck seemed to be on our side. The rain stung my face as waves roared. My brothers and I huddled in the very front of the boat, both to keep out of the rain and also to help keep the nose of the boat down. With the winds and the waves, Dad couldn't get the boat up on plane. It was horribly inefficient, and we were burning through fuel.

I clung to the sides of the boat as Dad yelled to me, "Jim, go check the gas tank! I am afraid we are not going to make it on this tank."

I crawled to the back of the boat, and shook the tank, nearly empty. We were still in the middle of the open water. "Dad, I it's pretty empty. I don't think we will make it"

"Okay, I was afraid of that. Stay there. If the engine stops, quickly change to the other tank. Do it as fast as possible, and don't forget to prime the gas line. I don't want to be out here without power."

My heart pounded as I gripped the gas line, waves crashing over us. My hands shook, stomach knotting, as I gripped the gas line. If I took too long, we could easily capsize. No one would be see it and we would likely drown.

The engine sputtered a few times and then shut off. The boat stopped moving and the waves started crashing over the bow. I didn't wait to be told. I pulled the gas line from one tank and pushed it onto the other. I frantically pumped the ball on the gas line to push fuel from the tank to the engine.

I screamed, "GO! New tank connected."

Dad turned the key, the engine turned over, but didn't start. I pumped the fuel ball a few more times. He tried again. Still, it did not start. I was beginning to panic, but I had a job to do. I pumped that gas bulb as quickly as I could. Dad tried it a third time, and the engine started.

Dad yelled, "Get back up front! We need as much weight as we can get up there."

We made it back. The boat was beached and tied, then we ran back to camp, but we looked like drowned rats. Shivering in soaked clothes, we exchanged wide-eyed glances, hearts still racing from our narrow escape.

Tonsillectomy - Mom

Three boys are FUN, but along with the fun comes all kinds of surprises!! Some of those surprises are medical in terms of first-aid-type injuries. This story isn't about one of these, although there were certainly a lot of those!

This story is about a medical adventure that I never expected. Dr Sands was our doctor. He knew all of us "inside and out". When Jimmy was six and Donnie and Ronnie were five years old, Dr. Sands said they all needed their tonsils out. He had a brilliant idea! Let's do all three of them at the same time!

His reasons for the three surgeries made sense to us. Jimmy had bad tonsillitis and needed his adenoids taken care of. Donnie had frequent ear infections along with tonsillitis. Ronnie had frequent tonsillitis and bronchitis. The surgeries would reduce the number of antibiotic shots they were getting.

So we totally trusted Dr. Sands and scheduled all three surgeries at the local hospital. Oh yes, we were scared, but that was during the time that we thought doctors walked on water and we didn't question them.

The day before the surgery, they saw Dr. Sands for a pre-op. As he was examining them, he said, "We can't do surgery!" Oh no! After preparing the boys with books, pictures, and conversations about being in the hospital, we had to cancel the surgeries. Donnie had the mumps, and of course, the other two would get them! The operations were rescheduled for when they would all recover from the mumps.

That was about fifty-five years ago. I have never forgotten the surgery morning! All three boys reacted differently to the injections they were given before the surgeries. It was so scary!! Jimmy's face flushed a bright red. I think it was Donnie who went to sleep. Ronnie was active and restless. I couldn't get to each of them fast enough to calm them! I was running from boy to boy!

They put them each in their own crib-type bed so they could wheel them into surgery. They couldn't even be together! Then they wheeled them individually down a hall. I couldn't follow them through those double doors! Each of my babies was standing in their bed and holding onto the rails while crying for their mommy! I was watching through the little windows in the double doors. My tears flowed, and I thought, "What was I thinking? Will I get my babies back, and will they be ok?"

The wait was a form of torture. After the surgeries were over and they were brought back to their individual rooms, I went from boy to boy to console them. Again, they all reacted differently to the anesthesia, so it was very scary to me. I was told they would be fine, but I was overloaded with worry.

They all did 'okay', but I had my hands full with three small boys recovering from surgery. Of course, the ice cream helped!! The first night they were home, I heard gurgling in Donnie and Ronnie's room. Ron was coughing up blood! I thought he would bleed to death! He had a blood clot that was stuck in his throat. Yes, we survived, but I'm not sure it was the wisest thing to do surgery on all three boys at the same time.

I know that now the doctors don't do "routine" tonsillectomies. I know now that doctors make mistakes. I learned that it's okay to question their decisions. But my boys are in their 60s and thankfully survived that adventure. Reflecting on their ordeal brought back memories of my own tonsillectomy years earlier.

I had my tonsillectomy at nineteen. Frequent tonsillitis had left my throat raw, and I trusted Dr. Sands to fix it. Post-surgery, my throat throbbed as he leaned in, his voice low, confessing the scarring had turned a routine procedure into a dangerous ordeal. I suppose I could have bled out on the table. My heart sank, realizing the risk I'd unknowingly faced. That moment should have sparked doubts about his judgment with my boys, yet I clung to my unwavering trust in him.

PET SNAKES - JIM

My mom taught elementary school on Fort Huachuca, where she wrangled kids of military folks alongside her best friend Bonnie. Plenty of stories came from those days, but this one kicks off a few more. One day, she told me that a naturalist had visited her school, and she mentioned that he was touring the classrooms. She said she prepped her kids, saying, "I don't want anyone to complain, say yuck, or gross. He may let you pet the snake, but you don't have to."

She described how the naturalist showed up at her classroom with desert critters, including a couple of snakes. He held a five-foot-long one, explaining its habitat and diet, then grinned and asked, "So would Mrs. Selvy like to hold a snake?" The kids went wild, cheering her on.

Mom told me she wasn't one to back down, but snakes weren't her thing. Remembering what she'd told the kids, she'd painted herself in a corner. She eyed the naturalist and asked, "It won't bite, will it?"

"Oh no, she's tame. Her name is Ginger," he said. To show the kids she was fearless, she nodded and agreed. The naturalist draped the snake across her arms, and the kids squealed, thrilled to see their teacher with a snake. I can imagine the parents' stunned faces at dinner when their kids told the tale.

The naturalist was stunned, too—no teacher had ever said yes before. A couple of weeks later, he offered Mom a smaller snake as a class pet, teaching her how to feed it and clean its cage. She became a legend among the school kids. I'm not sure if the other teachers shared the children's enthusiasm.

At the end of the school year, when Mom got her classroom snake, the naturalist reached out about the snake she'd held. He asked if she would like it. It was too big for her classroom, so Mom grinned and said, "This snake's perfect for my birthday!" My birthday is in May, so it worked out. He provided a cage large enough for her.

So I got a snake for my birthday. I was a high school kid, thrilled to join the only other guy I knew who had a snake like mine—a Sonoran Gopher Snake, a non-venomous snake species. I learned that gopher snakes are often mistaken for rattlesnakes. Their heads differ, but their markings look similar. To ward off predators, mine would puff up, curl into a strike pose, and even rattle her tail like a rattlesnake, though she had no rattle. It usually fooled them. They're beneficial, eating mice, rats, lizards, baby snakes, and even rattlesnakes, so they shouldn't be killed. Instead, they should be relocated if they're a problem. As constrictors, they coil around prey, squeeze to stop breathing, and swallow it whole.

Ginger stayed calm, never hissing, even when I fumbled with her cage. The only time Ginger got fierce was when I dropped a mouse in her cage. She'd dart forward, eyes locked, ready to strike. She would hunt it and swallow it whole.

To relax, I would sit in the recliner reading a book or watching TV. Ginger would wrap her body around my shoulders and neck, resting her head on my glasses. She would rest against my skin, soaking in the warmth of my body. She never moved until I would get up to get a drink of water or put her back in her cage.

Outside, I would ride my bike around the neighborhood, wrapped up against the cold. She enjoyed being outside in the sun. One day, after I came back from a bike ride, Mom was talking with a lady at our front door. I mumbled an excuse, squeezing past to grab a glass of water, sweat still beading from my ride. She looked at me, saw Ginger, and screamed. She ran through our house, a house she had never been in, trying to find a way out. It was so funny. I still don't know who she was. I never saw her again.

Mom always brought home work from school. She needed some help at home, so we got a house cleaner. She would come one day a week while we were at school and work. She was a very hard worker. She didn't speak English too well, but well enough to get by.

She was never very comfortable with snakes in our house. At the time, we had up to five: two gopher snakes, a hog-nosed snake, a racer, and a kingsnake. She always claimed, "You got them poisonous snakes in there." Mom always reassured her that none were poisonous. It is illegal to possess most poisonous reptiles, including rattlesnakes, without proper permits. Exotic venomous snakes such as cobras and mambas, are explicitly prohibited.

Occasionally, a snake would get out. When it happened, the whole family got involved to find the wayward reptile. I remember one time the screen on Ginger's cage pulled back in the corner. She got out. We found her wrapped up in the dryer.

One night, Sam was not in his cage. Sam was the other gopher snake. He was only about a foot long. He was a character and not nearly as tame as Ginger. We knew the cleaning lady was coming the next day. We looked high and low for him, but never found him.

Mom and Dad discussed whether to tell her that Sam was missing. They decided not to. We couldn't find him, so she wouldn't accidentally stumble on him. At least that was the justification.

Well, my brothers and I came home from school. There was an empty bucket at the end of the driveway, a trail of soapy water to the open back door. The cleaning lady was nowhere to be seen. My brothers and I searched the house. In Mom and Dad's bedroom, the dresser was pulled from the wall. We still can't figure out how she moved it. It was VERY heavy and cumbersome. Curled up against the wall was Sam. We snatched him up and put him back in his cage.

Later that night, after Mom got home, the cleaning lady called. I don't know what she had to say, but Mom said she was scared and not coming back.

TROT LINE - JIM

As dusk fell, it was getting late, and Grandpa wanted to run his trotline at Okemah Lake. If you don't know what a trotline is, it is a fishing line anchored at both ends with multiple hooks attached at intervals along its length. The lines and hooks are heavier than what is commonly used on a fishing pole. It is baited with small fish or other larger bait to attract catfish primarily.

On this particular occasion, it was just he and I. The rest of the family was getting dinner ready. We were racing against the setting sun as we pulled up to the floating milk jug marking the end of the trotline. Grandpa pulled on the jug and the connecting cord to pull the hooks to the surface. We were using large chunks of smaller fish we had caught, along with beef liver. The line was hooked to the side of the boat as we ran down the line to prevent it from sinking to the bottom.

Grandpa's hands moved steadily as he baited a hook, the line attached to the boat slipped, and an unbaited hook caught him in the forearm. The hooks are much larger than normal. The barb pierced the meat of his arm, pushing through and out the other side. Blood spurted from his arm. He couldn't pull the hook back the way it went in because of the barb, and couldn't push it through because the hook was still connected to the trotline.

I reconnected the line back onto the boat so it wouldn't pull on his arm. His voice stayed steady as he said, "Jim, go get the wire cutters out of the tackle box."

I retrieved the pliers and handed them to him. He cut the hook from the trotline. When the line was no longer connected, he was able to push the rest of the hook all the way through his arm. Blood still sprayed, staining the side of the boat.

Grandpa, ever the calm one, said, "Okay, I have to keep pressure on the wound. You are going to have to get us back. First, drop the trotline back in the water, then drive the boat back to the dock."

I dropped the line back in the water. It snapped as the line hit the water's surface, then sank to the floor of the lake. My hands shook on the throttle—I was only in elementary school at the time, and I don't think I had ever driven his boat. I know I had driven ours a few times, but always on open water. I was going to have to pull up to the dock. I had seen it done hundreds of times, but never done it myself. My chest tightened, knowing Grandpa was hurt, adding to the stress.

I took a deep breath, mimicking Grandpa's calm, and started the boat, swung it around, and headed back home. The engine's hum filled the silence as I pushed the boat as fast as I could. As I got close, I pointed the nose toward the dock at about a 45-degree angle. I pulled back on the throttle and let the wave push us in. The nose gently touched the dock. I jumped out, grabbed the rope, and tied the nose to the dock. I ran to the back and did the same.

Grandpa smiled, "That was perfect. You go ahead and collect the bait. We can't leave it here. I'm heading back to the trailer so Grandma can start cleaning this out. It looks like it is not bleeding as much now. I'll meet you there. Good job."

Looking back, it was a scary time for a young boy. As I steadied the boat, I realized that staying calm kept me focused; panicking wouldn't have helped. I learned a few things from the adventure.

First, Grandpa's steady voice taught me to keep calm in an emergency. Freaking out wouldn't have helped get what needed to be done.

Second, focus on what you can do, and don't worry about what you can't control. Grandpa pressed the wound while I steered us home. We each did what we could.

Third, you can do more than you think you can. I hesitated at the throttle, scared about docking the boat. I'd seen it done lots of times, but doing it myself was different. I didn't have a choice, so I just did it. Worst comes to worst, I could have beached the boat and worried about docking later.

The sun was dipping low when Grandpa gathered us for his favorite fish fry at Okemah Lake. He loved having family around, and the fish fry event was the day's highlight. We spent all day catching perch and crappies, water skiing, and swimming. The dock bustled with laughter and splashing nets. At day's end, we helped clean the fish, slicing them into small pieces and packaging them in plastic bags for freezing.

As the sun sank, we gathered for the main event. Grandpa fired up the cooking oil and battered the fish for deep-frying. I don't know the exact recipe, but I should ask my cousins for it. What I do remember is that it called for beer. Our family wasn't big on alcohol, so Grandpa's special trip to the store for a six-pack felt like an adventure.

As an adult, I don't care for beer. Fresh beer smells good, but the flavor doesn't do anything for me. But in the fish batter, it was great. It gave it a taste of hops. I didn't know what that was at the time. It caused the batter to puff up, making the fish pieces light and airy.

On this day, my family arrived late at the lake. Grandpa was trudging up from the dock, grinning wide, carrying a HUGE channel catfish. It thrashed fiercely, unhappy out of water. He'd caught it on a trotline hook. Its slick skin gleamed under the sun. It was about the size of a medium-sized dog. We weighed it, and it was over twenty-two pounds.

Grandpa hauled the fish to the large double sinks for cleaning and tossed it in. It flopped and flopped, slapping the steel with wet thuds. This three-foot-long giant was destined for our family's dinner.

Grandpa filleted it into steak-sized pieces, each slice as thick as a book. I'd never seen such massive fish portions. After discarding the carcass and packing the fillets into plastic bags, we headed back to the trailer. Fish was the star tonight, and plenty for all.

Grandpa cut some fillets into bite-sized chunks, dipped them in the beer batter, and deep-fried them. The golden pieces crackled as they hit the plate, filling the air with a savory aroma. The crispy batter melted in my mouth, bursting with flavor. That one catfish fed us for several cookouts.

BOAT SNAKE - DON

My grandparents had a boat dock at Okemah Lake, and I loved our trips there. After skiing or fishing, we'd tie up the boat, race up the hill, and dig into Grandma's sandwiches or hot stew. Grandpa had a ton of rules, but the big one after fishing was to clear all bait from the boat. I made sure any minnows I used were off the hook and tossed into the water. We always searched the boat to make sure no bait was left on the floor.

I don't remember whose fishing pole it was, but a dried minnow hung from a forgotten hook. As Grandpa untied the boat, my brothers Ron and Jim and I climbed in and took our seats. My heart skipped when

I caught a twitch in the boat's shadow. I froze, eyes locked on it, and then—bam!—I saw it: a snake! I vaulted across the boat, scrambling onto the dock, hollering, "Snake!" My voice cracked like a whip in the quiet air.

Ron and Jim bolted from the boat, nearly stumbling over each other in a chaotic scramble. I stood on the dock, pulse racing, watching them trip over their own feet. Grandpa, cool as ever, eased into the boat, his shoes creaking on the deck. Slowly but surely, he made his way to where I'd been sitting. Sure enough, there was a snake, a Water Moccasin, writhing and coiled, thrashing helplessly on the boat's floor.

Grandpa leaned in, squinting, and spotted the snake tangled on the fishing pole's hook. A hook was in the snake's mouth, and it couldn't dislodge it. A dried-up minnow dangled on the hook next to the snake's jaws. I realized the snake had slithered into the boat, lured by the minnow's scent, and chomped down. My stomach churned imagining that thing near my feet just moments ago.

Once Grandpa was sure the snake was securely hooked, he snatched the fishing pole's handle, hopped onto the dock, and whipped the snake in a wide arc over the lake. I held my breath as he sliced the line with a quick flick, sending the snake, minnow, and hook sailing into the lake. I let out a nervous laugh, relieved it was gone.

I learned a hard lesson that day: always double-check the boat and fishing lines for bait. One forgotten minnow nearly gave me a heart attack!

DOG POO - JIM

We moved to Arizona in the summer of
1974. In the fall, I was starting 7th grade
in junior high. It was a three-year school.
Though 9th grade was considered part
of high school, it was at the junior high
campus. The high school campus only
had 10th through 12th grades.

By 1975, we began our annual summer
treks to my mom's parents in Oklahoma.
Usually, Dad came along, but that year,
work kept him in Arizona. So, Mom, my
brothers Ron and Don, and I piled into our
small four-door brown Datsun. It already
smelled of old snacks and dog hair. But a
week of grandparent-fueled fun awaited.

I slouched in the front seat, savoring our summer freedom while Dad slaved away.

We brought our dogs along, including our German Shepherd, Mickey, a sixty-pound marvel. She was a fantastic dog. Mom had trained her in obedience, even winning competitions. Mickey was a seasoned traveler, never causing trouble on our road trips. But in Amarillo, Texas, our luck ran dry.

Halfway to Oklahoma, the Texas heat baked the interstate, shimmering off the asphalt. Suddenly, Mickey unleashed a silent-but-deadly gas attack. The stench hit like a punch, a rancid cloud trapped in our car with the windows sealed against the summer swelter. I clutched my nose in the front seat, gasping. "Ugh! I can't breathe. It's like a sewer exploded in my face!" I groaned.

Don yelled, "Pull over, Mom! I'm gonna puke!"

Mom, eyes scanning for road, said, "Can't yet. Nowhere to pull over. I'm looking for an exit."

Ron and Don cracked their windows, desperate for relief. The breeze helped, but the funk clung to us like a bad memory.

Then Ron shouted, "Mom, her tail's up again! Do something! She's gonna blow!"

"I'm trying!" Mom snapped, gripping the wheel.

She wasn't fast enough. Mickey unleashed a pile of diarrhea, a putrid explosion that coated the back seat. The smell was a nightmare, ten times worse than before. We gagged in unison, trapped in a rolling stink bomb.

Mom swerved into a gas station. She yanked Mickey out to 'go potty', but the damage was done. We attacked the mess with paper towels, scrubbing with water from the air station's hose. I gagged as the soggy towels smeared the chaos more than cleaned it. The seat was still damp, so we layered towels over it, praying it'd hold until Oklahoma.

Don complained, "This car's never gonna smell right again."

I'll never forget that sixty-pound dog, tail high, turning our car into a mobile biohazard disaster zone on that scorching interstate. We still laugh about the 'Amarillo Stinkocalypse'. A childhood memory I'd rather not relive, but it never fails to crack us up.

4TH OF JULY - JIM

Grandma and Grandpa had some land out in the country. It was a great place for my brothers, cousins, and me. They often had over the whole gang, but especially on the holidays.

I remember the hot days of the Fourth of July, playing all day long. We boy cousins all ran around in shorts with no shirts. You gotta feel sorry for the poor girl cousins. More often than not, we didn't even wear shoes. As the day wound down, our parents would call us in for dinner. It was a family affair. Each of the families brought or made things for the shindig. There was always too much food.

Our favorite dessert was Grandma's Wacky Cake[1]. The family has the chocolate cake recipe, but the frosting recipe is lost. It was made with cocoa powder and cooked down enough so that when poured onto the cake, it would set hard, almost like melted chocolate chips. It was delicious. I always thought Wacky Cake was a strange name growing up. I later learned online that it was created during the Depression. It was made without milk, eggs, or butter, scarce during the Depression and wartime.

But, being the Fourth of July, watermelon was always available. I remember all the cousins standing on the porch, eating the juicy, sweet melon. It was probably a good thing we were not wearing shirts, because the juice ran out of our mouths, down our chests, and onto our bellies. We didn't have seedless melons back then, and what fun would that have been anyway? We had seed spitting contests. The spitting added to the red juice running down our bodies.

After dinner and cleanup, the excitement turned to fireworks. These fireworks were not like today's. Everything was dangerous, even the sparklers. The sparklers were metal with a flammable coating. When the coating ignited, the heat traveled down the metal, often burning our hands.

I guess the black snake[2] firework was not too dangerous. You lit them with a match, and they expanded to look like a snake growing. But the real fireworks were what we wanted. I don't know if it was an abundance of caution or their own desire to have fun, but our fathers normally lit the real bang fireworks. I remember the dangerous example they set.

My uncle would say, "Now don't ever do this." He held the firecracker in one hand, lit it with the other, and tossed it. One time, they had some small ones called Lady Fingers[3]. One had a short fuse. My uncle lit it and tossed it very quickly. It exploded less than twelve inches from his hand. This was my youngest uncle, Phil, then unmarried and childless.

Ski Vortex - Jim

Dad gripped the wheel of our blue and white boat, its engine roaring as it pulled us across the lake for water skiing. My brothers and I smiled, whooped, and waved as we skimmed the water. Ever the showoff, I carved wild zigzags and raced to the wake to jump and get air. The wind whipped my hair as I leaned into each turn, my brothers cheering when I caught big air, only to splash back down with a stinging slap. Light as feathers, we sprang atop the water the moment Dad slammed the throttle, the boat's wake spraying our faces.

I learned to use two skis. To graduate to slalom skiing, using one ski, I would start on two skis to get up on top of the water, step out of one ski, leaving it floating in the water, and move the foot into the strap at the rear of the remaining ski. Mastering that trick, I wobbled but steadied on one ski, gaining confidence before tackling a full stop-start. Gliding on one ski felt smoother and less clumsy than kicking off the second mid-ride.

We sprawled on the boat's vinyl seats, the leather hot against my legs, passing around a bag of chips while Dad revved the engine for Mom's turn. The boat's engine hummed as we settled in, watching Mom leap into the water, her slalom ski gleaming. The lake shimmered under the noon sun, ducks squawking overhead as we prepped for another run. The sun blazed, sparkling off the glassy lake. She glided effortlessly at first, her ski slicing clean arcs.

Then Dad's eyes glinted, a sly grin spreading as he cranked the wheel counterclockwise. The boat carved a medium-sized circle, and Mom's hand chopped the air, signaling to straighten out. He didn't. After two loops, the wakes piled up, waves swelling, troughs deepening. Mom's legs wobbled, her arms strained against the rope, her face twisting in a grimace. She shouted, "Go straight!" but Dad just chuckled. Finally, she flung the tow rope skyward, flipped Dad the bird, and sank into the water with a splash. As Mom sank into the water, I grinned, knowing these lake days were memories I'd carry forever. I could still hear my brothers' laughter from earlier runs, their voices blending with the lapping waves, etching this day into my heart. I know Mom still remembers it, but I am not so sure it's as funny as I do.

We all laughed, but I bet Dad slept on the couch that night.

SURPRISE - JIM

When I started junior high, we moved to Arizona. The next summer, Grandpa and Grandma took all the grandkids to a local theme park outside Oklahoma City called Frontier City. We were invited, but we were too far away, so we couldn't go. Aunt Jo and Grandpa pleaded weekly for us to join them at the park.

My parents planned a secret trip to surprise our relatives at Frontier City, taking us kids with them. Mom and Dad huddled over maps in the kitchen, whispering about Frontier City, then packed us kids into the camper for a surprise reunion. We traveled to Oklahoma in our camper, the camper's engine humming as we rolled through

Oklahoma's flat highways, dust coating the windows while my brothers bickered over who got the top bunk, and checked in at the RV park associated with Frontier City. We made camp, had some dinner, and bedded down for the night. I was so excited for the next day's surprise that I tossed and turned all night. In my bunk, I imagined Grandpa's shocked smile, my heart thumping so loud I feared it'd wake everyone.

Grandpa, with his trusty wristwatch and park map, always led the charge at dawn to beat the crowds and maximize our fun. We schemed to saunter past the park's entry line, ready to grin or wave the moment a cousin spotted us. We were eager to time how long it took for a cousin to pick us out of the crowd. My brothers and I bet on which cousin would spot us first, stifling giggles as we pictured their shocked faces.

The five of us in my family calmly strolled the line heading to the back like we were getting in line. The park buzzed with cotton candy scents and roller coaster screeches, my sneakers crunching on gravel as we joined the entry line. We were able to pass all of them before my cousin Angela said, "Was that Aunt Sharon?"

We stopped and looked back. They turned around to see what Angela was talking about. Their jaws dropped, stunned faces lit up, and eyes wide rewarded every moment I'd held my tongue.

Cousins mobbed us with cheers and hugs, Grandma's eyes twinkled, while Aunt Jo's sobs stole the show, her voice choked with joy. Mom nudged me, whispering, "Look at Jo, she's been wiping tears of joy all day!"

My brothers and I spent the whole day with the cousins, riding the rides at the park. The Hammer sent my stomach soaring with every loop, my brothers and cousins screaming in unison, our laughter echoing as we raced to the next ride.

ROCKY POINT - JIM

I can still feel the crunch of sand under my sneakers from those childhood camping trips to Puerto Peñasco—Rocky Point—100 miles from Arizona down a potholed, two-lane road that rattled our old pickup camper. Back then, the Gulf of California lapped at a raw, untamed shore, home to weathered fishermen who sold us boxes of frozen shrimp for pennies. No condos, no restaurants, just endless dunes and salty air stinging my nose.

We parked our camper as the tide pulled back, leaving volcanic tide pools glinting under the sun. Don, Ron, and I darted across the jagged rocks, our fingers prying into crevices for shells and anemones. Their slimy tendrils pulsed against my touch, vibrant pinks and greens shimmering in the water. We were fearless, lost in discovery, while Mom's laughter and Dad's clanging pots echoed from the camper's tiny kitchen. Sharks? Unheard of in those shallow pools. We were boys from the desert who didn't know about the ways of the ocean. But tides, I learned, don't stay out.

Don and I felt the water's chill creep up our ankles and scrambled back to shore. Ron lingered, perched on a barnacle-crusted rock, his eyes glued to a pool's depths. Waves began to swirl, frothing around his sneakers. "Ron, get back here!" I shouted, my voice sharp against the ocean's roar.

Mom sprinted from the camper to the water's edge, her calm words barely masking panic. "Ron, hurry, the tide's coming in." Her hands gripped the hem of her shirt, knuckles white.

Ron's head snapped up. His rock was now an island, waves licking higher, foam bubbling over his feet. The volcanic rocks, slick and uneven, were treacherous even without the tide. Now, with the ocean surging, each step was a gamble. He hesitated, then plunged a foot into the churning water, gripping a jagged outcrop for balance. The waves slammed his legs, greedy, trying to drag him down. He stumbled, his knee smacking rock, but he hauled himself up, salt-streaked hair plastered to his forehead.

I held my breath, fists clenched, as Ron inched forward. A wave knocked him sideways, his arms flailing, but he found his footing on a patch of sand, steadying himself. Step by step, he battled the tide's pull, the ocean hissing and spitting. Mom's voice urged him on, a lifeline in the chaos.

Soaked, shivering, Ron staggered onto the beach, his chest heaving. We rushed him, relief flooding us like the tide itself. That moment, his trembling grin, the ocean's roar, burned into my memory. An adventure etched in salt and survival.

Christmas at Rocky Point meant piling into our pickup camper with our girl cousins, the Gulf of California's salty breeze whipping through the open windows. The rough, two-lane road from Arizona shook us for

100 miles, but the promise of adventure kept our spirits high. We parked on the beach, the same rugged shore as always, but heard whispers of a nearby beach with softer ground, less sand, more mud.

I stepped onto that new beach, and my feet sank into cool, squishy mud that oozed between my toes. Tufts of wiry grass poked through the surface, and every so often, a bubble gurgled up and popped with a faint hiss. My cousins and I, six kids total, crouched low, staring as the mud seemed to breathe. "Mussels," an adult declared, pointing to the bubbles. "Something's living down there."

The mussels were black, shiny, and half the size of my hand. Someone handed us pails, and we dug, mud caking our fingers, laughter echoing as we unearthed a haul. We soaked the mussels in fresh water, rinsing off the sludge, and packed them for later, our buckets brimming.

Back at our cousins' home on the Indian Reservation, where their parents ran the school as principal and teacher, we met up with our Oklahoma cousins. Nine kids total, we turned the house into a playground, chasing each other through the halls, our voices bouncing off the walls, music playing on a record player someone got for Christmas. The mussels hit boiling, salty water, steaming alongside traditional Christmas fixings, turkey, potatoes, and pies. I tried a few mussels, chewing their tough, rubbery flesh, but at that age, I wasn't the bold eater I've since become. Still, the table buzzed with chatter, plates clattering, and the joy of being together.

We stayed up late, sprawled on blankets, giggling over games and stories, the desert night cool outside. It was a Christmas of muddy hands and full hearts, one I can still taste when I think of those salty mussels.

Years later, we learned that muddy beach was often tainted with sewage. Eating those mussels wasn't our brightest move, but the boiling water must've killed anything harmful. No one got sick. Still, the lesson stuck: know where your food comes from. Those mussels, pulled from the muck, were a gamble we didn't know we were taking, but they made that Christmas unforgettable.

About the Author

James Selvy, a newcomer to writing, is a native of Arizona and a long-time resident of Tucson, where he spent 36 years supporting the troops in the defense industry. Now he writes the kind of stories he loves to read—where each journey is a chance to stretch yourself to become a better you.

With the steady hand of a technical mind his debut novel, Growing Up, is a testament to the power of family. When he's not scribbling stories, James is kept in line by his two wiener dogs and a Bernedoodle, or basking in the desert sun, dreaming up the next chuckle-worthy tale.

Follow author on Facebook: https://www.facebook.com/profile.php?id= 61576939872688#

Website: http://wolfpac-books-com

ENDNOTES

Boat Sunk - Jim

1. Oklahoma WIldlife Conservation http://www.wildlifedepartment.com/fishing/wheretofish/northeast/okemah-lake

2. American Red Cross, 7/8/2024 http://www.redcross.org/take-a-class/resources/articles/eating-before-swimming-myth

Suckers - Jim

1. WebMD 10/12/2023 http://www.webmd.com/skin-problems-and-treatments/prevent-treat-chigger-bites

4th of July - Jim

1. Amanda Rettke 3/30/2020 http://iambaker.net/depression-cake/

2. TNT Fireworks – Black Snakes snake fireworks Y o u T u b e https://www.youtube.com/watch?v=WA7fmAGfplo

3. Megabanger Fireworks – Landfinger Cracker 40's YouTube https://www.youtube.com/watch?v=iGll-xU8BuI

www.ingramcontent.com/pod-product-compliance
Lightning Source LLC
Chambersburg PA
CBHW021126130626
46554CB00002B/881